H. T. Allen

Allen's Illustrated Guide to Niagara

H. T. Allen

Allen's Illustrated Guide to Niagara

ISBN/EAN: 9783743442702

Manufactured in Europe, USA, Canada, Australia, Japa

Cover: Foto ©Andreas Hilbeck / pixelio.de

Manufactured and distributed by brebook publishing software
(www.brebook.com)

H. T. Allen

Allen's Illustrated Guide to Niagara

.

ALLEN'S

Illustrated Guide

TO

NIAGARA + FALLS.

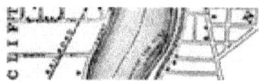

A MAP
of
THE VICINITY OF
NIAGARA FALLS
Drawn from Actual Survey
FOR
TUNIS' GUIDE
BY
J. H. FAIRBANK

NIAGARA—TABLE ROCK.

NIAGARA SUSPENSION BRIDGE.

REFERENCES

No. 1 Cataract, &c.   No. 6 Spencer House,
" 2 International,   " 7 Railroad Depots,
" 3 Goat Island Bridge, "   8 Park Place,
" 4 Niagara House,   "
" 5 Churches,

ILLUSTRATED GUIDE

TO

NIAGARA.

—————•—————

REVISED AND PUBLISHED BY H. T. ALLEN.

—————•••————

BUFFALO·
THE COURIER COMPANY, PRINTERS.

1881.

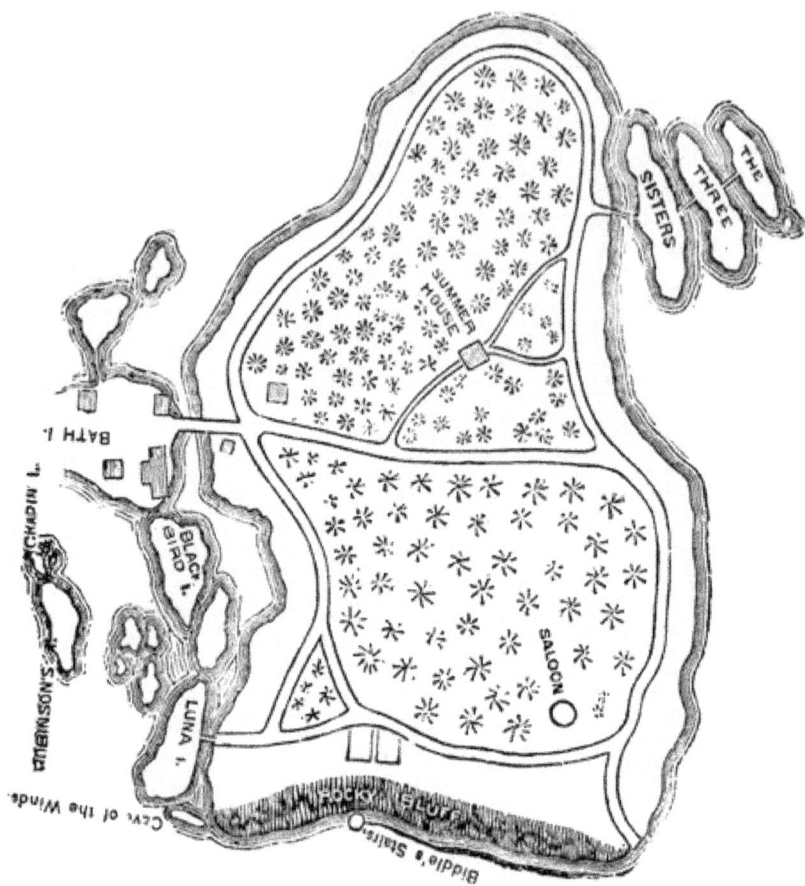

THE

THREE

SISTERS

SUMMER HOUSE

BATH I.

CHADIN I.

BLACK BIRD I.

ROBINSON'S

LUNA I.

SALOON

Cav. of the Winds.

ROCKY BLUFF.

Biddle's Stairs.

INDEX.

ILLUSTRATIONS AND MAPS.

GUIDE TO NIAGARA.

NIAGARA RIVER.

F the river itself much might be written, presenting as it does to the historian, the geologist
and the pleasure-seeker, an inexhaustible fund
of historical facts and incidents; an open book
for geological research, and a series of views which for
beauty and grandeur are unexcelled by any on the
American Continent. From the source of the river at
Buffalo, to Schlosser, a distance of twenty miles, it has a
fall of twenty feet, or an average of a foot to the mile.
Grand Island, twelve miles long and eight miles wide,
lies directly in the center of the river, the distance from
Buffalo to the head of the island, and from the falls to
the foot of the island, being the same. The waters thus
divided flow on, a grand and mighty river on either side,
until it becomes again united opposite Gill Creek, from
which point it assumes the majesty of an overwhelming
torrent, falling from Schlosser to the brink of the precipice, a distance of about three miles, fifty-three feet, in
its onward course falling over numerous little declivities,
forming as many pleasing little cascades, and anon
sweeping forward in fierce and turbulent rapids, as if
madly eager to make the awful leap into the seething

cauldron below. The river, as above by Grand Island, is here again divided by Goat or Iris Island, which division causes the formation of the two great cataracts, the American and Horseshoe Falls; again uniting at the foot of the island, after the awful plunge of one hundred and sixty-four feet, it sends up its bridal wreath of spray as if in token of a grand and harmonious reunion, oftentimes ascending to the height of a mile, appearing from a distance like the smoke of an immense conflagration, designating to the approaching tourist the location of this vast amphitheatre of struggling cataracts. From the foot of Goat Island to Lewiston, seven miles below, the river has a further fall of ninety-eight feet, from which point it flows grandly and serenely onward until its waters mingle with the unbroken swell of Lake Ontario.

The Historical associations that cluster around this wonderful river are innumerable. From the early war whoop of tribal contention through the long French and English wars to the closing of our own war of 1812–15, its borders have been the arena for many sanguinary conflicts, innumerable deeds of valor and strategy, through the long pioneer struggle for civilized existence, till the broad mantle of peace and Christian enlightenment settled smilingly down upon its borders, never again to be broken by the wild alarm of savage or civilized warfare.

The faces of the cliffs below the falls disclose an open page for the study of geology. The different strata underlying one another are well defined, and their variations at different points of the river present an interesting study, especially as this wonderful gorge lies directly in the center of the distinctive geological formation known as the "Niagara Limestone bed," the study of which has not been deemed unworthy by such minds as Lyell, Tyndall, Marsh and others.

The varied and delightful scenery of Niagara is fully described in the following pages of this Guide, it being the purpose of the writer to follow and describe each point of interest in rotation, as it would most naturally follow its predecessor in a complete tour of all the interesting points.

The map accompanying this work will be of great service to the Tourist, as it points out the relative position of the different points of interest.

GOAT ISLAND BRIDGE.

The old wooden bridge which had stood since 1818 was replaced by this costly and beautiful structure, in the summer of 1856. The foundations consist of massive oak timber cribs, filled with stone and covered with plates of iron. The superstructure is of iron, and consists of four arches of ninety feet span each, supported between the abutments of these piers. The whole length of the bridge is, therefore, three hundred and sixty feet, and its whole width is twenty-seven feet. Of this width a double carriageway occupies sixteen and a half feet, and two footways, one on either side of the carriageway, occupy, each, five and a quarter additional feet.

GOAT ISLAND BRIDGE.

No point commands so fine a view of the rapids as this bridge. The delicate tints of the water are here, especially, very attractive. The waves are breaking constantly into new forms, in each successive change catching the sunlight under new conditions, and throwing it back in some novel transfusion of hues.

It was while the old bridge was repairing, in the summer of 1839, that one of the workmen, a Mr. Chapin, was accidentally thrown from the frame-work into the river, and carried by the current to the first of the two smallest islands below, since called, from this circumstance, Chapin Island. He was thence rescued by the strong nerve and skillful hand of Mr. Joel R. Robinson, a man associated with many a gallant rescue from these waters.

The fall of the river's bed, from the head of the rapids to the verge of the precipice, is 58 feet. This gradual descent, by confusing the lines of vision as you gaze up the river, gives the farthest crest of the rapids a vague and skyish cast, suggestive of the Infinite; so that, turning from this to where the river disappears in its final leap, you seem to have realized in space the similitudes of life

"—— Standing 'twixt two eternities."

Crossing the bridge, the first island you reach is Bath Island. Looking up the Rapids, that small sentimental looking island on your left, is called "Lovers' Retreat;" the island just beyond that, Brig Island. That large building on your right is a paper-mill, said to be the largest in the State. Passing from Bath Island over a short bridge, you stand on

GOAT ISLAND.

This, though not the largest, is by far the most beautiful island in the Niagara. Long before it was bridged to the American shore, it was visited from time to time by the few to whom its attractions were of more potent consideration than the peril of reaching it. The late Judge Porter, who visited it in 1805, remembered having seen the names of strangers cut into the bark of a beech near Horseshoe Fall, with the subjoined dates of 1771, 1772 and 1779.

The island is now owned by the Porter family, to whom it was ceded by the State of New York in 1818. It derived its name from the circumstance of a Mr. Stedman having placed some goats on it to pasture. This was in 1770. The area of the island is sixty-one and a half acres; its circumference about one mile.

Three paths branch off from the road by which you ascend the bank, the middle one dividing the island into two nearly equal parts, the left leading to the head of the island, and the right (the one usually taken) to the American Fall. Following this path you are conducted through a colonnade of forest trees, with the Rapids at your right, over a space of eighty rods to the northwestern point of the island, called, by what process of association no mortal can tell,

HOG'S BACK.

It was while walking directly under this point that the lamented Dr. Hungerford, of West Troy, N. Y., was killed in the spring of 1839, by the crumbling of a portion of the rock from above. This is the only accident that has ever occurred at the Falls by the falling of rock.

AMERICAN FALLS FROM GOAT ISLAND.

A MAP of THE VICINITY OF

NIAGARA FALLS

Drawn from Actual Survey

FOR

TUNIS' GUIDE

BY

J. H. FAIRBANK

REFERENCES

No. 1 Cataract,   No. 6 Spencer House,
" 2 International,   " 7 Railroad Depots,
" 3 Goat Island Bridge, " 8 Park Place,
" 4 Niagara House,
" 5 Churches,

NIAGARA SUSPENSION BRIDGE.

Passing by a narrow foot-path down the bank, and crossing the short bridge at your right, you stand upon a lovely spot called

LUNA ISLAND.

On the northern edge of this island, a few feet above the precipice, is a spot of mournful memory. On June 21, 1849, the family of Mr. Deforest, of Buffalo, together with Mr. Charles. Addington, their friend, were viewing the scenery from this point. The party, in fine spirits, were about leaving the island, when Mr. Addington advanced playfully to Miss Annetta, the little daughter of Mrs. Deforest, saying, "I am going to throw you in," at the same time lifting her lightly over the edge of the water. With a sudden impulse of fear the startled child flung herself from his hands, and struck the wild current of the river. With a shriek, the young man sprang to her recovery, but before the stricken group on shore had time to speak or move, they had passed over the precipice. The crushed remains of the lately blooming and buoyant child were found in the afternoon of the same day in the Cave of the Winds; and a few days afterward, the body of the gallant but fated young Addington was likewise recovered and committed with many tears to the village cemetery. This is, perhaps, the most touching casualty that has ever occurred at the Falls.

Leaving Luna Island, pause for a moment at the foot of the path before you ascend, while we point you out an appearance which certain imaginative persons have been pleased to call the

THE THREE PROFILES.

These so-called profiles are formed by the inequality of projection in that portion of the precipice which is formed by the western side of Luna Island. The rock is adjacent to and almost under the American Fall.

THE CENTER FALL.

This is that portion of the American Fall which is cut off by Luna Island. Having now ascended the bank, and rested from your fatigue, pass on a few rods to the Cave of the Winds' dressing rooms and Biddle's Stairs.

BIDDLE'S STAIRS.

These Stairs take their name from the well-kown President of the United States Bank, Nicholas Biddle, Esq., at whose expense they were erected in 1829.

They are secured to the solid rock by ponderous iron bolts, and are said to be perfectly safe. The perpendicular height of the bank at this place is 185 feet; the staircase itself being eighty feet high, and consisting of ninety steps. From the stairs to the river there is a rude pathway; but it is seldom traversed, except for the purpose of angling, an art which, at the right time of the year, is here practiced with the happiest success.

In 1829, shortly after the completion of the stairs, the eccentric Sam Patch, of saltatory memory, made his famous leap from a scaffolding ninety-six feet high, erected in the water at a point between this and the Center Fall

From the foot of Biddle's Stairs, two paths lead in opposite directions, one toward the Canada, and the other toward the American Fall. The former has been obstructed by slides from above, and is not, perhaps, altogether safe. Taking the latter, a few minutes' walk brings you to the celebrated Cave of the Winds. If you have provided dresses, you here enter by a secure stairway.

CAVE OF THE WINDS

The formation of this cave was of easy process. The gradual wearing away by the water of the shaly substratum of the precipice has left the limestone rock above projecting at least thirty feet beyond the base, thus forming an open cave, over which falls in deep folds of azure the magnificent curtain of the Center Fall. The compression of the atmosphere by the falling water is here so great that the cave is rendered as stormy and turbulent as that of old Æolus himself, from whose classical majesty, indeed, it derived its first name—

ÆOLUS'S CAVE.

Gazing now below you at that delicate textured rainbow trembling in the angry surge, you will hardly fail to remember Byron's vivid description of the bow at the cascade of Velir. :

> " From side to side, beneath the glittering morn,
> An Iris sits, amidst the infernal surge,
> Like hope upon a death-bed, and, unworn
> Its steely dyes, while all around is torn
> By the distracted waters, bears serene
> Its brilliant hues with all their beams unshorn ;
> Resembling, 'mid the torture of the scene,
> Love watching madness with unalterable mien."

Ascending Biddle's Stairs, your course conducts you to the right, along the verge of the precipice. Observe how the bank is gradually wearing away, by slides of land and crumbling of rocks from its side. It was near these stairs that the crash occurred in 1843. The detached rock now lies at the foot of the staircase.

By the time you have reached the other side of the island you will be prepared to duly appreciate the estimate of its width, with which Dr. Goldsmith edified the ingenuous youth of his time. The width of the island from fall to fall is seventy-five rods. You ha··· by this time reached the southwestern corner of the island. Be seated in the arbor near by, if you please, and we will pay you the highest possible compliment to yourself, while gracefully acknowledging our own impressions of the scene, by—silence. There are many descriptions of the Falls; but they are all too lucklessly ··· to the *form* of their subject—oceans of sublimity falling into perilous depths of pathos. It may, however, be remarked in passing that, take whatever point of view we may, we find Nature here expressing herself in bold and beautiful antitheses; the Titanic strength and majesty of the cataract, and the soft grovy tendrils that bathe their verdure in its spray—the wild, distracted, maniac surge, and delicate rainbow shivering in its embrace—the whirlwind roar of falling floods, and the braided lullaby of lapsing streams. Niagara is all antitheses, all "contrasted charms!" This is commonly called the Horseshoe Fall, a name derived from the shape that the curve formerly assumed. The gradual wearing away from beneath, and falling down from above of the rocks, has changed the figure from that of a horseshoe to something now more nearly resembling that of a right angle.

The width of this fall is about one hundred and forty-four rods; its height, one hundred and fifty-eight feet. The depth of the water in the center, or deepest part of the stream, is estimated at twenty feet, and this was proven by the fact of the ship Detroit, which drew eighteen feet, passing over without touching.

HORSESHOE FALL BEFORE REMOVAL OF TOWER.

TERRAPIN BRIDGE.

This Bridge is subject to the action of the spray; a little care should therefore be taken in crossing it. In the winter of 1852, a gentleman from West Troy, N. Y., while crossing to the tower, fell into the current, and was carried to the verge of the fall, where he lodged between two rocks. He was discovered by two of the citizens, who rescued him by throwing out lines which he fastened around his body. He remained speechless for several hours after being taken to his hotel.

From this point you get the best view of the shape of the fall, and the clearest idea of how it has been modified by the action of the water. This action has been especially violent during the last few years. On Sunday, February 1, 1852, a portion of the precipice, stretching from the edge of the island toward the tower, about one hundred and twenty-five feet long and sixty feet wide, and reaching from near the foot to the bottom of the fall, fell with a crash of thunder. The next day another, a triangular piece, with a base of about forty feet, broke off just below the tower. Between the two portions that had thus fallen off, stood a rectangular projection about thirty feet long and fifteen feet wide, extending from the top to the bottom of the precipice. This immense mass became loosened from the main body of the rock and settled perpendicularly about eight feet, where it now stands, an enormous column one hundred and fifty feet high by the dimensions named above.

The line of division between the government of the United States and that of Canada is in the deepest part of the channel, or through the angular part of the fall.

HORSESHOE FALLS FROM BELOW.

Leaving the Horseshoe fall and wending our way along the bank of the river to the east, the next point of interest is the Three Sister Islands, connected by three beautiful bridges. These costly and substantial structures, built over the three channels which separate the Three Sisters from each other and from Goat Island, present new and grand views of the rapids and falls, unequalled from any other point. These three bridges combine both strength and beauty. They are alike, being slightly oval, that is higher in the middle than at either end, thus adding to their strength. The ends are fastened into the solid rock. Two rods, two inches in diameter, pass under each bridge and are also fastened in the rocks at either end. The peculiar construction of the railing adds much to their strength and beauty. Pass over each bridge slowly, and carefully view the rapids and cascades—views never before made apparent to the eye. Here Joel R. Robinson, in 1841, saved a Mr. Allen's life, and in 1854 he passed with his son over the rapids. From the head of the third Sister may be seen one continuous cascade for all, extending as far as the eye can reach, from Goat Island across to the Canada shore, varying from ten to twenty feet in height. From this miniature Niagara rises a spray similar to that of the great Falls. The rapids here are very fine, surpassing in volume the rapids under Goat Island bridge, and much more beautiful in appearance.

The pleasure of passing over these wild and romantic spots fully repays the visitor for the trip, to say nothing of the many other beautiful resorts that abound at Niagara, both winter and summer. A few rods further on, and you have reached the

HEAD OF GOAT ISLAND.

This point commands a comprehensive view in outline of the river and its environs for some miles of its course. Looking up the right bank, you behold, at a distance of about a mile, a small, white farm house, with a chimney of most disproportionate size. This is a site of old Fort Schlosser, a name celebrated in border story. That towering chimney was taken entire from the mess-house attached to the establishment. This fort was built at an early date by the French, and called by them Little Fort. At the end of the Anglo-French war in America it was ceded to the English, and was first occupied as a military post by Captain Schlosser, from whom it derived its second name. One mile above Schlosser is Schlosser Landing. In a diagonal direction from this point, and near the Canada shore, is

NAVY ISLAND.

This island has an area of 304 acres, and belongs to the realm of Her Britannic Majesty. It is closely associated with Schlosser by an affair which, as it has not yet found its way into the pages of Bancroft or Hildreth, we will briefly relate : In 1837, a rebellion was stirred up against the authorities of Canada, by some disaffected "Radicals," under the leadership of Wm. Lyon McKenzie and some others ; but, Her Majesty's subjects not caring to side with the "Rebels" in any great number, the movement was speedily put down. But not so the leaders. They—*i. e.* McKenzie, Gen. Sutherland, and five and six and twenty others—at the suggestion of Dr. Chapin of Buffalo, unfurled the standard of rebellion over this island, designing to make it a *rendezvous* for the restless

patriots of both sides of the river, until sufficient strength.
should be gained to renew the attack.   Matters were
going on pleasantly—the "Patriots" being daily edified
by accessions to their strength, though greatly demoral-
ized by a barrel of whiskey that found its way to their
panting hearts—when the difficulty of "transporting
volunteers and supplies to their place of destination,"
and "the number of persons, from motives of business
or curiosity constantly desirous of passing and repassing
from the main-land to the patriot camp, suggested to
Mr. Wells, the owner of a small steamboat lying at
Buffalo, called the Caroline, the idea of taking out the
necessary papers, and running his vessel as a ferry boat
between the American shore and the islands, for his own
pecuniary emolument."   Accordingly, Friday, December
29, the Caroline left Buffalo for Schlosser; and after
having arrived, having made several trips during the day,
on account of the owner, was moored to the wharf at
Schlosser Landing during the night.

Colonel Allan McNab, then commanding at Chippewa
a detachment of Her Majesty's forces, having got word
of the enterprise of the Caroline, resolved upon a deed
which relieves the farcical story of the rebellion by a
dash of genuine daring.   It is asserted that Sir Allan
was informed that the Caroline was in the interests
of the Patriots, chartered for their use, and intended
to act offensively against the Canadian authorities.
Whether this be true or not, he planned her destruc-
tion that very night.   For this purpose a chosen band
is detailed and placed under the command of Captain Drew, a retired-on-half-pay officer of the royal
navy.

At midnight the captain received his parting orders from Sir Allan, and the chivalrous band departed in eight boats for the scene of their gallant daring.

The unconscious Caroline, meanwhile, lay peacefully at her moorings, beneath the stars and stripes of her country's banner. As the tavern at Schlosser—the only building near by—could accommodate but a limited number of persons, several had sought a night's lodging within the sides of the boat. Dreaming of no danger, they had retired to rest unprovided with arms. Thus was the night wearing on, when so stealthily came the hostile band that the faint splash of muffled oars was the first intimation that the sentry had of their approach. In reply to his question, "Who goes there?" came, first "*Friends!*" then a heavy plashing in the water; then, the leaping of armed men to the deck. The bewildered sleepers start from their dreams and rush for the shore. "Cut them down!" shrieks the heroic Drew, as he thrills with the memory of Aboukir and Nile—"Cut them down, give no quarter." More or less injured, they escape to the shore, with life—all but one, Durfee, the last man to leave, who is brought to the earth by a pistol shot, a corpse!

A few minutes and the Caroline moves from the shore in flames! Down the wild current she speeds faster and faster, flinging flames in her track, till striking the Canada waters she spurns the contact, leaps like a mad fury, and in a moment more is as dark as the night around her. The common account of this affair takes it for granted that the boat went over the Canada Fall aflame. You will read of the fated vessel lifting her fairy form to the verge of the precipice, lighting up the dark amphitheatre of cataracts, etc., to the end of endurance. The case was far otherwise. The physician who was called to the wounded at Schlosser was riding up the river's bank while the Caroline was descending the rapids. The gentleman testifies that the boat, a perfect mass of illumination, her timbers all aflame, and her pipes red hot, instantly expired when she struck the cascade below the head of Goat Island.

GRAND ISLAND

Lies not far above Navy Island, is twelve miles in length, and from two to seven in breadth. The land is highly fertile, and much of it is in actual state of cultivation. It was on this island that the late Major Mordecai M. Noah, of New York, designed to build the "City of Ararat," as a place of refuge for the scattered tribes of Israel. In 1825, he even went so far as to lay the corner stone, amid infinite pomp, and to erect a monument commemorative of the occasion. The monument is still standing, in excellent state of preservation.

At the foot of this island lies Buckhorn Island, with an area of about 300 acres. Between these two islands is an arm of the river, deep and clear, called

BURNT SHIP BAY,

From a circumstance connected with the close of the French war of 1759. The garrison at Schlosser had already made a gallant resistance to one attack of the English and were preparing for another, when, disheartened by the news of the fall of Quebec, they resolved to destroy the two armed vessels containing their military stores. Accordingly they brought them to this bay and set them on fire. The wrecks, even at this day, are sometimes visible.

BROCK'S MONUMENT AND RIVER BELOW LEWISTON. (See Page 42.)

PROSPECT PARK.

Following the course of the river from Goat Island Bridge toward the precipice, a short walk brings you to the entrance of Prospect Park. These grounds, comprising what are familiarly known as the "Ferry Grove" and "Point View," were purchased by the Prospect Park Company in 1872. A carriage road leading from the entrance runs along the edge of the rapids to the brink of the Falls. A solid wall of masonry guards this spot, and from the angle can be obtained a magnificent view of the American Falls and the frowning rocks below, and continues along the bank of the river to the new Suspension Bridge, enabling persons to get a view of the American Falls, Goat Island, Horseshoe Falls, Table Rock, Clifton House, the Ferry and the new Suspension Bridge, without stepping from their carriage. Cool, shady walks run in all directions, and rustic seats at intervals invite the visitor to linger here and gaze at the magnificent scenery spread out before him. The Park Company have also erected a beautiful pavilion where visitors can "trip the light fantastic toe" within sound of the roar of the great Cataract. An elegant restaurant is also in the grounds, where they can regale the inner man when tired of sight-

AMERICAN FALLS FROM BELOW.

seeing. From the Ferry House, near the center of the grounds, you can descend through a cut in the bank to the water's edge, a distance of 360 feet. The spiral stairs, constructed here in 1825, having become shaky with age, the present novel but commodious contrivance was inaugurated in 1845. The flight of steps leading along the railway consists of 290 steps. The car is drawn up the inclined plane by water-power—an over-shot wheel being turned by a stream diverted from the river for that purpose. Around a wheel eight feet in diameter, which turns in a horizontal position at the head of the railway, runs a cable two and a half inches in diameter and 300 feet in length, attached to a car at either end, and supported by pulleys placed at convenient intervals down the grade. At the foot of the stairs, turning to the left, the company have erected a commodious and substantial building, from whence may be obtained, from the base of the descending torrent, one of the most magnificent views of the Falls. A view which the visitor should in no case fail to see. Here, also, during the afternoon when the skies are bright and the direction of the wind is down the river, the spectator may behold a marvelous picture by "Nature's own cunning hand," in colors of red, orange and violet, reflected and refracted by the spray beads of the ascending clouds. A passage has been made by which visitors may pass under and behind the American Fall as far as their inclination will prompt.

CROSSING THE RIVER.

The advisable course, we think, is to cross the river at the Ferry in going, and at the Suspension Bridge in returning. The best time for crossing at the Ferry, in

FRONT OF CAVE OF THE WINDS.

summer, is either in the morning, or two or three hours before sunset. If the light is favorable—and in summer, at these hours, it almost always is—this crossing will probably afford you your most vivid and lasting impression of the Falls. Nowhere d you have so fine a view of the Falls as *from below*. For from the base of the stupendous cataract, looking up to its towering crest, one gets a better idea of its grandeur and sublimity, the eye better appreciates the distance (one hundred and seventy-five feet) from below than when looking into its depths, and the feeling of disappointment which some experience when they first behold the Falls, vanishes as they gaze upon them from this spot.

You may here test in your own experience the worth of Burke's æsthetic principle with regard to height and depth. "I am apt to imagine [Burke on the Sublime and Beautiful, §8] that height is less grand than depth, and that we are more struck at looking down from a precipice, than looking up at an object of equal height; but of that I am not very sure." This was a necessary result of connecting the feeling of the sublime with that of self-preservation. We doubtless feel more of *terror* (are more "struck") in looking down a depth than up a height; but terror, so far as being a principle, or even a condition of sublimity, cannot for a moment co-exist with its nobler forms.

The voyageur who crosses here may be led to ask the depth of the river. From the latest U. S. survey we are enabled to give the actual figures. The actual depth near the center, between the Ferry stairs and the landing place on the Canadian side, was found to be 192 feet. If we take into account the vast mass of rock and shale that ages ago was hurled into the river's bed when the

FALLS FROM NEW BRIDGE.

Falls were at this point, it is not unreasonable to suppose
that then its depth was far greater—at least fifty feet. To
show the extreme depth of the mighty trench Niagara has
made from the crest of the Falls to the original bed of the
river, must be some 420 feet. The mighty engine that
still slowly performs this gigantic task, is Niagara's flood
descending with resistless force, a distance of 420 feet,
with the weight of 2,000,000 tons per minute.

Carriages await you at the landing on the Canada side.
The distance up the bank from the water's edge to the
Clifton House is 160 rods. Proceeding from the Clifton
House along the bank toward the Canadian Fall, the first
object to arrest your steps is

THE MUSEUM.

This collection of natural and artificial curiosities is
well worth seeing. The galleries are arranged to repre-
sent a forest scene, filled with beasts, birds and creeping
things. There are, besides, several chained-up ferocities
in the yard, and a tastefully arranged green-house in the
garden.

A few rods below the Museum, Miss Martha K. Rugg
fell from the bank while attempting to pick a flower that
grew on its edge. She was living when reached, but
expired soon afterward. The accident occurred August
24, 1844.

TABLE ROCK

Is about twenty rods above the Museum, at the angle
formed by the Horseshoe Fall with the Canadian bank.
The bank here sends out, far beyond the line of its
general perpendicular, a regular table-like ledge of rock,
in the same plane with the crest of the cataract.

FALLS FROM CANADIAN SIDE.

The form and dimensions of Table Rock have been changed by frequent and violent disruptions. In July, 1818, a mass broke off 160 feet in length, and from thirty to forty feet in width. December 9, 1828, three immense portions, reaching under the Horseshoe Fall, fell " with a shock like an earthquake." In the summer of 1829, another large mass fell off, and June 26, 1850, a piece 200 feet long and sixty feet deep. Those who wish to go under the Horseshoe Fall can descend a road cut from the museum to the foot of the fall. Dresses can be procured and guides obtained to pass under Table Rock.

It was on Table Rock that Mrs. Sigourney wrote her spirited

APOSTROPHE TO NIAGARA.

Flow on forever, in thy glorious robe
Of terror and of beauty. God has set
His rainbow on thy forehead, and the clouds
Mantled around thy feet. And He doth give
Thy voice of thunder power to speak of Him
Eternally :—bidding the lip of man
Keep silence, and upon thy rocky altar, pour
Incense of awe-struck praise.

                And who can dare
To lift the insect trump of earthly hope,
Or love, or sorrow, 'mid the peal sublime
Of thy tremendous hymn ! Even ocean shrinks
Back from thy brotherhood, and his wild waves
Retire abashed ; for he doth sometimes seem
To sleep like a spent laborer, and recall
His wearied billows from the vieing play,
And lull them to a cradle calm : but thou,
With everlasting, undecaying tide, .
Dost rest not night nor day.

              The morning stars
When first they sang o'er young creation's birth,
Heard thy deep anthem ; and those wrecking fires
That wait the archangel's signal, to dissolve
The solid earth, shall find Jehovah's name
Graven, as with a thousand diamond spears,

On thine unfathomed page. Each leafy bough
That lifts itself within thy proud domain,
Doth gather greenness from thy living spray,
And tremble at the baptism. Lo! yon birds
Do venture boldly near, bathing their wings
Amid thy foam and mist. 'Tis meet for them
To touch thy garments here, or lightly stir
The snowy leaflets of this vapor wreath,
Who sport unharmed on the fleecy cloud,
And listen to the echoing gate of heaven
Without reproof. But as for us, it seems
Scarce lawful with our broken tones to speak
Familiarly of thee. Methinks, to tint
Thy glorious features with our pencil's point,
Or woo thee with the tablet of a song,
Were profanation.

THE BURNING SPRING

Is reached by one of the most charming and picturesque
drives in this vicinity. Starting from Table Rock, the
road leads across Cedar Island, along the foaming rapids,
over two handsome suspension bridges, connecting at
either extremity "Clark Hill Islands" with the mainland.

The spring is about one mile above the Falls, near the
head of the rapids, which are second only to the Falls,
and here the view is grand. The water moving at the rate
of near forty miles an hour, together with the wonders of
the Spring, makes it an interesting place for the tourist.

The water of the Spring is highly charged with sul-
phuretted hydrogen gas, and emits a pale, blue light when
ignited. To heighten the effect, the phenomenon of the
burning water is exhibited in a darkened room. Near this
spot was fought the battle of Chippewa, July 5, 1814.

LUNDY'S LANE BATTLE GROUND

Is one mile and a half westwardly from the Falls. On
this plain was fought the great battle of the war of 1814,
July 25. The loss on both sides, in killed and wounded,
was nearly 1,800. The village near by is Drummondville,
in memory of Gen. Drummond, the commander of the

2

British forces on the line.   From this point we return and
recross to the American side l y

THE NEW SUSPENSION BRIDGE,

One-eighth of a mile below the American cataract, opened
to the public on the fourth day of January, 1869.   It is
the longest suspension bridge in the world, its roadway
being 1,300 feet in length.   Its cables are 1,800 feet in
length; the towers 100 feet high, and it spans the mighty
chasm through which rolls its floods towards Lake
Ontario, 190 feet above the water.

From this bridge the most delightful views of the Falls
are to be obtained, as well as of the great ravine between
the Canadian Fall and the Rapids, a distance of two
miles, along the bottom of which the vast drainage of
the upper inland seas flows in a stream 250 feet in
depth.   It is but a walk of twenty minutes from the
principal hotels on the American side to the former site
of Table Rock and the Horseshoe Fall on the Canada
side.

As a work of engineering art and mechanical skill, it
adds new attraction to the scenery which excites the
admiration of every beholder, and is indeed the envy of
all other nations.

SUSPENSION BRIDGE

Is two miles below the Falls, is 800 feet long, and extends
230 feet above one of the most turbulent streams on the
globe.   It is owned by a stock company, and cost about
500,000 dollars.   It was built under the superintendence
of J. A. Roebling.   The cars of the Great Western Railway pass over the bridge to connect with the New York
Central.

NEW SUSPENSION BRIDGE.

The following are the dimensions :

Length of span from center to center of towers	822 feet.
Height of tower above rock on the American side	88 "
" " " " " Canada side	78 "
" " " " floor of railway	60 "
" " track above water	258 "
Number of wire cables...............................	4
Diameter of each cable	10⅝ in.
Number of No. 9 wires in each cable...............	3,659
Ultimate aggregate strength of cables	12,400 tons.
Weight of superstructure	800 "
" " " and maximum loads	1,250 "
Maximum weight the cable and stays will support..........	7,309 "

NOTE.—The wires were first got across by means of a kite.

WHIRLPOOL RAPIDS.

This wonderful spot is about two miles distant from the Falls, down the rushing, green river, which, flowing at a profound depth between high banks, looks so quiet yet sullen, after leaving the howling abyss at the foot of the Falls. But at Whirlpool Rapids ! what a change ! The whole force of the water concentrates itself here, and seems as though it would tear asunder the steep, wooded banks that inclose it, so wild and startling is its terrific power; as far as the eye can reach the water thunders down in seething, heaving masses of foam, throwing up streams of water covered with spray, and in places whirling it up into angry billows twenty or thirty feet above the heads of the spectators standing on the shore. It is deafening in its roar, and here, even more than at the brink of the Falls, can we have a realization of the terrific force of Niagara.

At this point an elevator has been built, worked by a water-wheel some 300 feet below the top of the bank, enabling the visitor to reach the water's edge without fatigue.

RAILWAY SUSPENSION BRIDGE

Through a channel but about 300 feet in width, and walled-in by giant banks, from the summit of which it makes one giddy to look down, rush the gathered waters of Lakes Superior, Michigan, Huron, St. Clair and Erie! Those who have descended to the river's edge, gazed upon the wild tumultuous surge, and listened to its roar, can form. some idea of this mighty mass of struggling waters. No description can do it justice. Exaggeration itself is baffled.

The depth of the water at the Rapids is estimated to be not less than two hundred and fifty feet! The natural inquiry on reading the above would be: "How did you happen to find that out?" The answer is: We know about the amount of water (very nearly) passing over the Falls, the rapidity with which it runs, and the width of the river at this point—hence the calculation is easily made, nor may the conclusion reached be characterized as a far-fetched or very erroneous one.

In fact the river *must* be very deep, as the visitor will readily comprehend, to admit the passage of this immense volume of water.

At this point, on the sixth day of June, 1861, occurred one of the most daring feats ever attempted by a human being. The little steamer *Maid of the Mist* left her moorings, about a quarter of a mile above the Suspension Bridge, June 6, 1861, and swung boldly out into the river, to try one of the most perilous voyages ever made. She shot forward like an arrow of light, bowed gracefully to the multitude on the bridge, and with the velocity of lightning passed on to meet her doom. Many beheld this hazardous, daring adventure, expecting at every instant she would be dashed to pieces and disappear

WHIRLPOOL RAPIDS.

forever. Amazement thrilled every heart, and it appeared as if no power short of *Omnipotence* could save her. "There! there!" was the suppressed exclamation that escaped the lips of all. "She careens over! She is *lost!* She is *lost!*" But, guided by an eye that dimmed not, and a hand that never trembled, she was piloted through those maddened waters by the intrepid Robinson in perfect safety, and is now performing less hazardous voyages on the St. Lawrence.

She is the only craft, so far as we know, that ever made this fearful trip and lived. Though our intrepid hero had performed many hazardous exploits in saving the lives of persons who had fallen into the river, yet this last act, in taking the *Maid of the Mist* through the Whirlpool, is the climax of all his adventures. The boat lost her smoke-stack, but otherwise received no injury, being very strongly built.

Three men were on board, Pilot, Engineer and Fireman, all safe.

A short distance further down stream we find the Whirlpool, which is a vast basin or amphitheatre, with an ill-proportioned opening at right angles with the river above; this opening is to the right as you have your back to the Falls, and is comparatively narrow. The pool is shut in on all sides, save the opening mentioned, by rocky cliffs 350 feet high, whose sides facing the river are quite smooth and perpendicular. The basin containing the pool is nearly circular, and together with the waters form a very picturesque scene. But as to the pool itself it must be acknowledged that many are disappointed with its appearance. It is not in the shape of a vast caldron or pool formed by an outlet in the bottom of a vessel, whereby the center is greatly depressed, etc., but, on the contrary, the pool in question is actually ten feet higher in the center than at the sides; it is formed by the pent-up, agitated waters, in their bewildered course to find an outlet, terrifically "swinging round the circle." I can illustrate in nowise more plainly than to compare the river to some ferocious animal who, having never known defeat, has suddenly, by his own carelessness, fallen into a trap. His first impulse is to walk round the outer edge of the pit, that he may find a means of escape. This passage when found appears to be wholly inadequate, and yet it has answered for thousands of years. Facilities for seeing the Whirlpool are afforded by an inclined railway on the Canadian side, and by a most romantic stairway on the American.

Less than half a mile further down the river, on the American side, is the Devil's Hole, a terrible gloomy and savage chasm in the bank of the river, between one and two hundred feet deep   Overhanging this dark cavern is a perpendicular precipice, from the top of which falls a small stream, usually dry in summer, named the "Bloody Run."

LEWISTON.

On the twenty-fourth of May, 1798, Surveyor-General De Witt wrote to Mr. Ellicott, of the Holland Land Company, "to examine where a town could most conveniently be placed on the Niagara River, where the Indian title had been extinguished," and to "furnish a map and survey thereof." Mr. Ellicott recommended Lewiston as the place; and surely a prettier, or at the time more eligible site, could not have been selected. It is seven miles below the Falls, nestling at the foot of the mountain amid a wealth of "living greenness"—the very

ideal of rural loveliness.   As the head of navigation on
the lower Niagara, it is a place of considerable importance, but has been much injured by the construction of
the Erie and Welland canals.   It contains, besides a pro-
portionate number of stores and hotels, churches of all
the various denominations, and an academy of considerable size.   In 1812, it was the head-quarters of Gen. Van
Rensselaer, of the New York militia.   Here may be seen
the remains of the third Suspension Bridge erected at
this place and destroyed.

QUEENSTON

is a small village opposite Lewiston, containing about 200
inhabitants, three churches—Episcopal, Presbyterian and
Baptist—a telegraph office and a tannery.   The name of
this place is associated in history with the gallant defense
by the British of the adjacent heights, in the war of 1812.
The village is prettily situated, but its importance has
been lessened by the same causes which have retarded
the growth of Lewiston.

BROCK'S MONUMENT.

On Queenston Heights, just above the village of this
name, near the spot where the gallant soldier fell, stands
a monument to Gen. Brock, beneath which his ashes and
those of his aid-de-camp, McDonald, repose.   The first
monument was completed in 1826, and consisted of a plain
shaft of freestone, about 126 feet high, and surmounted
by an observatory, reached by a spiral stairs on the inside
This was blown up by some miscreant, on the night
the 17th of April, 1840.   The present structure—
urated Aug. 13th, 1853, amid the enthusiasm of over

10,000 people present—is far more magnificent than the former. Its w 'e height is 185 feet. The sub-base is forty feet square and thirty feet high. On this are placed four lions, facing respectively north, south, east and west. Next is the base of the pedestal, twenty-one feet six inches square, and ten feet high. Then comes the pedestal, sixteen feet square and ten feet high, bearing a heavy cornice, ornamented with lion-heads alternately with wreaths in alto-relievo. From the top of the pedestal to the top of the base of the shaft, the form changes from square to round. The shaft is a fluted column of freestone, seventy-five feet in height, and ten feet in diameter, surrounded by a Corinthian capital, ten feet high, on which is worked in relief a statue of the Goddess of War. Then comes a round dome, nine feet high, which is reached by 250 spiral steps from the base on the inside. The whole is surmounted by a massive statue of General Isaac Brock.

FORT NIAGARA

Is built at the mouth of the Niagara River on the American side. Within the last few years, important repairs have been made around the fort, and the entire wall has been constructed anew. " During the progress of these repairs, many relics of former days were found. The entrances to the several underground passages were discovered; but owing to their ruinous state, they were not entered; could this have been done, no doubt many interesting discoveries would have been made." This spot is interesting as historic ground, when associated with the memory of the heroic La Salle, and the gentle and courtly De Nonville, and all the gallant "chiefs and

ladies fair " that have graced its frowning walls.   The
village adjacent to the fort is called Youngstown, from
the name of its founder, the late John Young, Esq.
Here was fought the battle of the 24th of July, 1759, in
which Prideaux, the English general, fell, and after which
the French garrison surrendered to Sir William Johnson,
who succeeded to the command of the English.

NIAGARA,

Opposite Youngstown, is one of the oldest towns in Upper Canada, and was at one time the capital of the prov-
ince.   It is on the site of the old town of Newark, burnt
by Gen. M'Clure, December 10th, 1813.   It is a pleasant
town, facing Lake Ontario on one side, and the river on
the other.   In former days, its importance was much
more considerable than at present.   Since the completion of the Welland Canal, St. Catharines, being more
centrally situated, has absorbed its trade, and detracted
very much from its prosperity.

A short distance above the village are seen the ruins
of old Fort George, taken by the Americans, under Dearborn, May 29th, 1813, destroyed by M'Clure, December
10th, and has never been rebuilt.   A little below the
town is Fort Mississaga, where a detachment of British
soldiers is stationed.

WINTER SCENE AT NIAGARA FALLS.

NIAGARA IN WINTER.

COMPARATIVELY few persons know anything of the indescribable grandeur of Niagara in winter. "No one truly appreciates Niagara who has not seen it in winter. Deeply as the manifold grandeur and beauty of its summer aspect impress the beholder, and solemn and delicious as are the emotions it inspires when arrayed in the rich drapery of autumn, it is still more impressive when clad in the superb and dazzling livery of winter.

"There is at this time a universal bleakness which repels the vision from discursive movements, and concentrates it, with overwhelming effect, upon the brilliant spectacle of the cataract itself, and certainly that spectacle is among the most striking and splendid of earthly scenes.

"Its wonderful enchantment is chiefly due to the gradual freezing of the spray, blown thinly over the islands and adjacent shores, until the simplest objects assume the most grotesque or significant forms, shaped in transparent ice. Very marvelous is the change to one who stood by that majestic tide in the bright hours of August

or October. The islands that were then carpeted with
verdure, and beaming with the soft tints of summer, are
now laid in ice as pure and solid as the most stainless
Parian; while the trees and shrubs, that so lately blazed
with the splendors of autumn, are robed in the same
spotless vesture, and borne down to the very ground by
its massy weight. Even the giant rocks, that shoot up so
boldly from the far depths of the precipice, are hooded
and wrapped with vast breadths of ice, as if to rebuke
their fantastic impertinence. All things are encased and
enveloped with gleaming ice. Ice islands are covered
with forests of ice that bend down to the ice with the
iciest of fruits. Everywhere, but in the immediate channel of the swollen and surging river, the ice-giant reigns
sovereign of the ascendant.

"One of the most singular effects of this frosty domin-
ion is displayed upon Luna Island (of beautiful memory),
where the trees are bowed down to the earth with their
snowy vestments, like so many white nuns doing saintly
homage to the genius of the place. But the most magnificent and bewitching effect is produced by the morning
sun when it pours over these fairy-like islands and forests
a flood of kindling rays. At such a moment the charac-
teristic attributes of Niagara seem fused and heightened
into 'something more exquisite still.' Its intrinsic sublimity and beauty experience a liberal transfiguration.
Nature is visibly idealized. Nothing more brilliant or
enchanting can be conceived. The brightest tales of
magic 'pale their ineffectual fires.' Islands, whose flowers
are thickset diamonds, and forests, whose branches are
glittering with brilliants, and amethysts, and pearls, seem
no longer a luxurious figment of genius, but a living
and beaming reality One feels in the midst of such

blazing coruscations and such glorious bursts of radiance, as if the magician's ring had been slipped upon his finger unawares, and, rubbed unwittingly, had summoned the gorgeous scene before him. It is as if Mammoth Cave, with its groves of stalactites, and crystal bowers, and Gothic avenue and halls, and star chambers, and flashing grottoes, were suddenly uncapped to the wintry sun, and bathed in his thrilling beams; or as if the fabled palace of Neptune had risen abruptly from the deep, and were flinging its splendors in the eye of heaven."

It is indeed a scene of peerless grandeur, and would richly repay a pilgrimage from the extremest limits of the nation. A man of taste and feeling should be willing to "put a girdle round the globe" to witness it. We are amazed that parties of enterprising tourists do not flock there from all quarters of the Union. They surely have little passion for the sublime and beautiful who think of the scene only to shudder at it and forego it.

NIAGARA FALLS BY MOONLIGHT.

There is much the same difference between Niagara in the "gairish light of day" and Niagara bathed in the soft splendor of moonlight, that there would be between the Paradise Lost in the freedom of its epic grandeur and the same translated into vapid prose. The peculiar charm of the scene is not in the separate enjoyment of the silvery light and of the forceful flood, nor yet in any contrast between the grace of the one and the strength of the other, but in the instantaneous blending of complimentary influences, a sort of "gladness in accomplished promise." The peculiar effect of moonlight upon the features of a landscape is to harmonize, to soften, to spiritualize. Everything within its smile is lighter and more graceful. The rivers are turned into "vales of winding light;" the cliffs lose their harshness of outline; the trees, in their picturesque repose, look like the trees of a dream; even sound itself, in sympathy with the scene, falls upon the ear with softer cadence. A favorite haunt at Niagara in this magical season is Goat Island. It is here that the best views are obtained of that rare phenomenon, the Lunar Bow. At the time of the full moon this exhibition is as perfect as lunar light can make it. At best, however, it is very faint, a mere belt of the saintly hue. Many persons consider the lunar bow a sufficient justification of immoderate raptures; but its attractiveness, we cannot but think, is owing more to its being so seldom seen than to any intrinsic beauty it may possess.

THE FIRST MAN WHO SAW THE FALLS.

The first white man who saw the Falls, so far as we have any authentic record, was Father Hennepin, Jesuit missionary, sent out from the French among the Indians, as early as the year 1678—200 years since. His descriptions were visionary and exceedingly exaggerated. He thought the Falls six or seven hundred feet high, and that four persons could walk abreast under the sheet of water without any other inconvenience than a slight sprinkling from the spray. But we would not attribute this wild and fanciful description to a want of candor, or an intention to deceive. The fact probably was, he had no means of measuring its height, and undoubtedly got his account from the Indians, which very likely would be incorrect.

The most graceful rhymes indigenous to the, locality are the following by the late Colonel Porter, who was an artist both with the pencil and the pen. They were written for a young relative in playful explanation of a sketch he had drawn at the top of a page in her Album, representing the Falls in the distance, and an Indian chief and two Europeans in the foreground:

" An Artist, underneath his sign (a masterpiece, of course),
Had written, to prevent mistakes, ' This represents a horse ;'
So, ere I send my Album Sketch, lest connoisseurs should err,
I think it well my Pen should be my Art's Interpreter.

" A chieftain of the Iroquois, clad in a bison's skin,
Had led two travelers through the wood, *La Salle* and *Hennepin*.
He points, and there they, standing, gaze upon the ceaseless flow
Of waters falling as they fell two hundred years ago.

" Those three are gone, and little heed our worldly gain or loss—
The Chief, the Soldier of the Sword, the Soldier of the Cross.
One died in battle, one in bed, and one by secret foe ·
But the waters fall as once they fell two hundred years ago.

" Ah, me ! what myriads of men, since then, have come and gone ;
What states have risen and decayed, what prizes lost and won ;
What varied tricks the juggler, *Time*, has played with all below :
But the waters fall as once they fell two hundred years ago.

" What troops of tourists have encamped upon the river's brink ;
What poets shed from countless quills, Niagaras of ink ;
What artist armies tried to fix the evanescent bow
Of the waters falling as they fell two hundred years ago.

*   *   *   *   *   *   *   *

' And stately inns feed scores of guests from well replenished larder ;
And hackmen drive their horses hard, but drive a bargain harder ;
And screaming locomotives rush in anguish to and fro :
But the waters fall as once they fell two hundred years ago.

" And brides of every age and clime frequent the island's bower,
And gaze from off the stone-built perch, hence called the Bridal Tower ;
And many a lunar belle goes forth to meet a lunar beau,
By the waters falling as they fell two hundred years ago.

3

"And bridges bind thy breast, Oh, stream! and buzzing mill-wheels turn,
To show, like *Samson*, thou art forced thy daily bread to earn;
And steamers splash thy milk-white waves, exulting as they go:
But the waters fall as once they fell two hundred years ago.

"Thy banks no longer are the same that early travelers found them,
They break and crumble now and then like other banks around them;
And on their verge our life sweeps on—alternate joy and woe:
But the waters fall as once they fell two hundred years ago.

"Thus phantoms of a by-gone age have melted like the spray,
And in our turn we too shall pass, the phantoms of to-day;
But the armies of the coming time shall watch the ceaseless flow
Of waters falling as they fell two hundred years ago."

THE NIAGARA FRONTIER.

Niagara River, from lake to lake, comprehends a length of only about thirty-six miles. Contracted as this border region is, as an important section of the geographical lines between governments that have not always been on terms of amity, it has often been made the theatre of war. Its localities are therefore associated with the history of our country, and with the fame of her military chieftains, and on this, if on no other account, are worthy of a description. The history of this region discloses to our view, first, the lordly Indian, roaming the majestic solitude; next, the wary pioneers of the civilization and the vices of Europe, mingling the hereditary hatred of their respective nations when crossing one another's path; then, a protracted strife for the mastery between the delegated powers of the nations; then, a lull of peace and prosperity; again, the atrocities of war; and again, and now, the blessings of peace.

First, our immediate predecessors;

THE IROQUOI ˙

This was the name given by the French to the confederacy of the Five Nations, consisting of the Mohawks, on the river of that name, the Oneidas, on the southern shore of Oneida Lake, the Cayugas, near Cayuga Lake, and the Senecas, stretching from the Seneca Lake to the Niagara River. Father Hennepin says that there were villages of the Senecas on the Niagara not many miles above the Falls. The Iroquois Senecas were, therefore, the immediate predecessors of the whites on this frontier. Remnants of this once mighty people, whom Volney, in a burst of enthusiasm, called the ROMANS OF THE WEST, still linger round their primeval homesteads. The Tuscaroras, a tribe incorporated with the Iroquois in 1712, still enjoy the *reservation* of their lands, and occupy a village about nine miles from the Falls. The remains of the Senecas dwell further to the south. It is a curious fact, that, while the rapacity of the ɔhite man has stripped them almost entirely of their possessions, and shorn them of their power, their ancient league is still in force, their traditional customs still observed. Yearly they glide to their council-fire through the waving grain-lands of their once forest-home, like lingering spirits of the past, to banquet on the recollections of their traditionary greatness. From their ancient seat at Onondaga, the council-fire is transferred to Tonawanda. Here their representatives yet assemble and perform their ancient rites and ceremonies.

It must not, however, be inferred that the Iroquois Senecas were the original proprietors of the soil, or the first of whom we have any account. Just above the horizon of history flits the shadow of a great and peaceful tribe,

THE NEUTER NATION,

Supposed to be identical with the Kah-Kwas, "in whose wigwams the fierce Hurons and relentless Iroquois met on *neutral ground*." Father L'Allemant, in 1641 mentions distinctly "the easternmost village of the Neutral Nation, 'Ongniaarha' (Niagara), of the same name as the river." In the following year Charlevoix also mentions this people, and says that they were called "'neutral' because they took no part in the wars which desolated the country." Canada West was the seat of the "fierce Hurons." Situated between this warlike people and the Iroquois, the neutrality of the Kah-Kwas could not long be preserved. "To avoid the fury of the Iroquois they joined them against the Hurons, but gained nothing by the union." They fell victims to the furious power they sought to conciliate, and disappeared as a nation about the year 1643. To their seats, as we have said, succeeded the Senecas, who were in occupation of them when first visited by

THE EUROPEAN PIONEERS.

It is not known when this region was first visited by Europeans, though such an event was *possible* any time after the discovery of the St. Lawrence in 1534.

"French traders are said to have visited the Falls as early as 1610 and 1615, but there are no authentic accounts to confirm this statement." Side by side with the French trader came the missionary priest—first the humble Franciscan, and then the wary disciple of Loyola. Father L'Allemant, writing of the Neuter Nation from St. Mary's Mission in 1641, says: "Although many of our French in that quarter have visited this people to profit by their furs and other commodities, we have no knowledge of any who have been there to preach the gospel except Father De La Roch Daillon, a Recollect, who passed the winter there in the year 1625." This good father was probably the first European in Western New York, and even of him it is said "there is no evidence that he ever saw the Falls." In the fall of 1640, two missionary fathers, Jean de Breboeuf and Joseph Marie Chaumont, found their way to some part of this region, but if they saw the Falls they made no mention of them. In 1660, Ducreux wrote a work called "Historiæ Canadensis," and noted the Falls on a map; but the probability is that he took them from nearsay, as he makes no allusion to them in his narrative.

THE EXPEDITION OF LA SALLE

Robert Cavalier de La Salle, a native of France, set out for the new world in 1667. Following up the St. Lawrence, he explored Lake Ontario, and ascended to Lake Erie. La Salle had heard from the Indians of the majestic Ohio, and of the fertile regions beyond, and in the mind of this man was first formed the project of uniting Canada with the valley of the Mississippi by a chain of military posts. Presenting his plans in a memorial to his government, and obtaining a commission for the exploration of the Father of Waters, he set out on his expedition, in the fall of 1678, with a numerous band of followers, among whom was Tonti, the Italian, and Father Hennepin. Touching at the present site of Fort Niagara, he there established a trading post. Making the portage from Lewiston to Cayuga Creek, on the American side, the whole company improved the opportunity of viewing

the Falls. Good Father Hennepin was quite bowed
down beneath their grandeur. He is confident that they
are above six hundred feet high, and describes them as
"a vast and prodigious cadence of water, which falls
down after a surprising and astonishing manner, inso-
much that the universe does not afford a parallel." As
they purposed visiting the head waters of the Mississippi,
it was necessary first to build a suitable vessel to navigate
the upper lakes. Accordingly a vessel of sixty tons
burden was built at the mouth of the Cayuga Creek, on
the American side of the river, about five miles above the
Falls. The vessel was named the "Griffin," in allusion
to the arms of the Count de Frontenac, the early patron
of La Salle. On the seventh of August, 1679, amid the
firing of guns, and the singing of the *Te Deum*, the
Griffin lifted her sails to the breeze—the first keel to enter
the waters of the upper lakes.

THE EXPEDITION OF DE NONVILLE

When Champlain came out from France in 1603, he
unwisely made the Iroquois the deadly enemies of the
French, by actively co-operating with the Hurons against
them. This course of policy had been afterward pur-
sued as a tradition, and when the Marquis de Nonville
succeeded to the government of New France, in 1685, he
found himself involved in a war with the Iroquois, in
defense of his Indian allies of the west. He at once
resolved to attack the Senecas first, and to build a fort at
Niagara, where La Salle had left a trading post. "The
commandant of the French posts at the west were
ordered to rendezvous at Niagara, with their troops, and
the warriors of their Indian allies were in that quarter."

The French army set out from Montreal on the thirteenth of June, and reached Irondequoit, on the southern shore of Lake Ontario, on the twelfth of July. According to previous arrangements, the commandant at Niagara, with the re-enforcements from the west, reached Irondequoit in the same hour with the division of De Nonville.

After laying waste the country in his course, and taking formal possession of some of the principal villages of the Senecas, De Nonville dispatched a detachment to Fort Frontenac (Kingston), to communicate the result of the expedition, and with the rest of his force set out for Niagara on the twenty-sixth, which he reached on the thirtieth. "In three days," says he, "the army had so fortified the post as to put it in a good condition of defense in case of an assault." A detachment of one hundred men left here, soon fell beneath the combined attacks of disease and the Senecas, and the post was again deserted. De Nonville left Niagara on the second of August. La Hontan was ordered to take a detachment of troops, and accompany the Indian allies on their return to the west. Rowing up from the fort to Lewiston, they carried their canoes over the portage on the American side, and launched them again at Schlosser. Scarcely had they pushed their skiffs from the shore, when a "thousand Iroquois" appeared on the river's bank. It was under the terror of such a pursuit that La Hontan, with three or four savages, left the main body to catch a hurried glimpse of that "fearful cataract" which, in his trepidation, he describes as "seven or eight hundred feet high, and half a league broad."

The facts of De Nonville's expedition are woven into W. H. C. Hosmer's beautiful poem of "Yonnondio."

THE TUSCARORAS

The Tuscarora reservation is upon a mountain ridge in the town of Lewiston, about nine miles northeast of the Falls. Driven from their original seats in North Carolina by the aggressions of the whites, they migrated to New York in 1712, and became merged in the confederacy of the Iroquois. In the revolutionary war a part of them inclined to the English, and a part remained neutral. Such portions of the Tuscaroras and Oneidas as had been allies of the English in their flight from the total rout of Gen. Sullivan, embarked in canoes upon Oneida Lake, and down the Oswego River, coasting along up Lake Ontario to the British garrison at Fort Niagara. In the spring, a part of them returned, and a part of them took possession of a mile square upon the mountain ridge, given them by the Senecas. The Holland Company afterward donated to them two square miles adjoining their reservation, and in 1804 they purchased of the company 4,329 acres, the aggregate of which several tracts is their present possessions.

NIAGARA FRONTIER IN 1812.

President Madison's proclamation of war threw the whole frontier into consternation. The pioneers, unprotected by a sufficient force, and dreading the treacherous warfare of the British Indians, were ready to abandon their homes to the tender mercies of the enemy. The strong positions of the Americans were Buffalo and Fort Niagara; those of the British were Fort Erie and Fort George, a redoubt opposite Black Rock, a battery at Chippewa, another below the Falls, and the defenses on Queenston Heights.

On the eleventh of August, Major-General Van Rensselaer, of the New York militia, established his head-
quarters at Lewiston. On the thirteenth of October, he
determined to cross the river at Lewiston and take possession of Queenston Heights. The attempt was successful. Shortly after the occupation, General Brock arrived
with a re-enforcement of 600 troops, and in attempting to
rally them after their first repulse, was killed. His aid-
de-camp, McDonald, fell, likewise, by his side. Meanwhile, the British having received another re-enforcement,
the undisciplined militia of Van Rensselaer's rear division,
as they had not yet crossed the river, preferred to remain
where they were, although they were obliged to see their
gallant companions suffer a *total defeat*. This was the
chief event on this frontier, in the campaign of 1812.
On the twenty-seventh of May, 1813, General Dearborn
captured from the British, Fort George, at Newark, near
Niagara, at the mouth of the Niagara River.

After the British had withdrawn their regular force
from the frontier, M'Clure, the American general in command of Ft. George, wantonly burned the town of Newark,
leaving its homeless inhabitants exposed to the inclem-
ency of the season, evacuated the conquered territory,
and returned to his own side of the river. But retribu-
tion was at hand. The post evacuated by M'Clure was
soon occupied by Col. Murray with a force of five hundred British soldiers and Indians. Gen. M'Clure, feeling
perfectly secure of Fort Niagara, took up his head-quarters
at Buffalo. Col. Leonard, equally secure, slept in his
own house three miles above the fort. Thus it was that
the force of Murray, crossing the river before day-break,
at a point about four miles above the fort, called the Five-
3*

mile Meadows, surprised the garrison, and made themselves masters of the post.   Indian scouts left the main
body, like bloodhounds, to scent up their prey.   The
whole frontier was a scene of the most intense suffering.
Lewiston, Niagara Falls, Black Rock and Buffalo fell an
easy prey to the destroyer.   All fled who could, *the militia
frequently leading the van.*   It was a motley throng flying
from the torch and the tomahawk of an invading foe,
with hardly the show of a military organization to cover
the retreat.   Buffalo was burned to the ground on the
thirtieth of December.   But the campaign of 1814 was
destined to retrieve, as far as possible, the fortunes of
this.   The executive appointed Gen. Brown to the command on this frontier, associating with him Winfield
Scott, Gaines, Miller and others.   Then followed a brilliant succession of victories—the capture of Fort Erie,
the battle of Chippewa, the battle of Lundy's Lane, and
finally, the greatest of all victories, peace.

RETROCESSION OF THE FALLS.

The fact that in historic times, even within the memory
of man, the fall has sensibly receded, prompts the question, how far has this recession gone?   At what point
did the ledge which thus continually creeps backwards
begin its retrograde course?   To minds disciplined in such
researches the answer has been and will be, at the pre-
cipitous declivity which crosses the Niagara from Lewiston on the American to Queenston on the Canadian side.
Over this traverse barrier the affluents of all upper lakes
once poured their waters, and here the work of erosion
began.   The dam, moreover, was demonstrably of suffi-

cient height to cause the river above it to submerge Goat
Island and this would perfectly account for the finding
by Mr. Hall, Sir Charles Lyell, and others, in the sand
and gravel of the island, the same fluviatile shells as are
now found in the Niagara River higher up. It would also
account for those deposits along the sides of the river,
the discovery of which enabled Lyell, Hall and Ramsay
to reduce to demonstration the popular belief that the
Niagara once flowed through a shallow valley.

The physics of the problem of excavation, which I
made clear to my mind before quitting Niagara, are re-
vealed by a close inspection of the present Horseshoe
Fall. Here we see evidently that the greatest weight of
water bends over the very apex of the Horseshoe. In a
passage in his excellent chapter on Niagara Falls, Mr.
Hall alludes to this fact. Here we have the most copious
and the most violent whirling of the shattered liquid;
here the most powerful eddies recoil against the shale.
From this portion of the fall, indeed, the spray sometimes rises without solution of continuity to the region of
clouds, becoming gradually more attenuated, and passing
finally through the condition of true cloud into invisible
vapor, which is sometimes re-precipitated higher up. All
the phenomera point distinctly to the center of the river
as the place of the greatest mechanical energy, and from
the center the vigor of the fall gradually dies away
toward the sides. The horseshoe form, with the con-
cavity facing downward, is an obvious and necessary
consequence of this action. Right along the middle of
the river the apex of the curve pushes its way backward,
cutting along the center a deep and comparatively narrow groove, and draining the sides as it passes them.

Hence the remarkable discrepancy between the widths
of the Niagara above and below the Horseshoe. All
along its course, from Lewiston Heights to the present
position, the form of the fall was probably that of a
horseshoe · for this is merely the expression of the
greater depth, and consequently greater excavating
power, of the center of the river. The gorge, moreover,
varies in width as the depth of the center of the ancient
river varied, being narrowest where that depth was
greatest.

The vast comparative erosive energy of the Horseshoe Fall comes strikingly into view when it and the
American Fall are compared together. The American
branch of the upper river is cut at a right angle by the
gorge of the Niagara. Here the Horseshoe Fall was the
real excavator. It cut the rock and formed the precipice
over which the American Fall tumbles. But since its
formation the erosive action of the American Fall has
been almost nil, while the Horseshoe has cut its way for
five hundred yards across the end of Goat Island, and
is now doubling back to excavate a channel parallel to
the length of the island. This point, I have just learned,
has not escaped the acute observation of Prof. Ramsay.
The river bends; the Horseshoe immediately accom-
modates itself to the bending, and will follow implicitly
the direction of the deepest water in the upper stream.
The flexibility of the gorge, if I may use the term, is
determined by the flexibility of the river channel above
it. Were the Niagara above the Fall sinuous, the gorge
would immediately follow its sinuosities. Once suggested, no doubt geographers will be able to point out
many examples of this action. The Zambesi is thought
to present a great difficulty to the erosion theory, because

of th sinuosity of the chasm below the Victoria Falls. But assuming the basalt to be of tolerably uniform texture, had the river been examined before the formation of this sinuous channel, the present zigzag course of the gorge below the Fall could, I am pursuaded, have been predicted, while the sounding of the present river would enable us to predict the course to be pursùed by the erosion in the future.

But not only has the Niagara River cut the gorge—it has carried away the chips of its own workshop. The shale being probably crumbled is easily carried away. But at the base of the Fall we find the huge boulders already described, and by some means or other these are removed down the river. The ice which fills the gorge in winter, and which grapples with the boulders, has been regarded as the transporting agent. Probably it is so to some extent. But erosion acts without ceasing on the abutting points of the boulder, thus withdrawing their support and urging them down the river. Solution also does its portion of the work. That solid matter is carried down is proved by the difference of depth between the Niagara River and Lake Ontario, where the river enters it. The depth falls from seventy-two feet to twenty feet, in consequence of the deposition of solid matter caused by the diminished motion of the river. Near the mouth of the gorge at Queenston, the depth, according to the Admiralty Chart, is 180 feet; well within the gorge it is 132 feet.

In conclusion we may say a word regarding the proximate future of Niagara. At the rate of excavation assigned to it by Sir Charles Lyell, namely, a foot a year, five thousand years or so will carry the Horseshoe Fall far higher than Goat Island. As the gorge recedes it will

drain, as it has hitherto done, the banks right and left of
it, thus leaving nearly a level terrace between Goat
Island and the edge of the gorge. Higher up it will
totally drain the American branch of the river, the channel of which will in due time become cultivable land.
The American Fall will then be transformed into a dry
precipice, forming a simple continuation of the cliffy
boundary of the Niagara. At the place occupied by the
Fall at this moment we shall have the gorge inclosing a
right angle, a second whirlpool being the consequence of
this. To those who visit Niagara a few milleniums hence
I leave the verification of this prediction. All that can be
said is, that if the causes now in action continue to act,
it will prove itself literally true.*

HACKMEN AND GUIDES.

Complaints are frequently made by strangers of being
outrageously *gulled* by hackmen and guides. This com-
plaint is a general one, and there is no reason for making
it with peculiar emphasis at Niagara. The experienced
tourist will always settle the price beforehand, and so avoid
any unpleasant scene at the end of his trip. This pre-
caution, so regularly observed in all other matters, should
not be omitted in this: the *price* of a thing should be
known before we engage to *pay* for it. The usual charge
for carriages is two dollars an hour. The compensation
for the service of guides is less definitely fixed. Other
complaints of a less specific character are also often made,
such as, "a quarter is demanded at every corner," etc.
The truth is, no more money is asked here than else-

* The article on the " Retrocession of the Falls," was written by Professor
Tyndall, after a visit to this place.

where for an equal, or perhaps less amount of value received; but the greater part of the world are so much accustomed to consider a tangible material return as the only form of the *quid pro quo,* that they cannot understand how so gross an affair as money should enter into considerations of this kind, and consequently regret its expenditures the more keenly.

FRANCIS ABBOTT, THE HERMIT OF NIAGARA.

The history of this singular individual has been given in various forms, from the hurried compilation of a guide-book to the extravagance of a romance. We present you with what is known of him by all who lived in the village at the time of his residing here.

His first appearance at Niagara was in the afternoon of June 18, 1839. He was a young man then, tall and well-formed, but emaciated and haggard; of an easy and gentlemanly deportment, but sufficiently eccentric in appearance to arrest a stranger's gaze.

Clad in a long flowing robe of brown, and carrying under his arm a roll of blankets, a book, portfolio, and flute, he proceeded to a small, retired inn, where he engaged a room for a week, stipulating, however, that the room was to be, for the time, exclusively *his,* and that only a *part* of his food was to be prepared by the family. Soon after, he visited the village library, entered his name, and drew books. He also purchased a violin. At the expiration of a week he returned to the library, where, falling into conversation, he spoke with much enthusiasm on the subject of the Falls, and expressed his intention of remaining some time longer.

Shortly afterward he asked permission of the proprie-
tor of these islands to erect a cabin on Moss Island,
that he might live in greater seclusion than the village
afforded him.   Failing in his request, he took up his
abode in a part of a small log-house, then standing near
the head of Goat Island.   Here for nearly two years he
continued to live, with no companion but his dog, his
books and his music—blameless but almost unknown.
On this island, at hours when it was unfrequented by
others, he delighted to roam, heedless, if not oblivious of
danger.   At that time a stick of timber about eight
inches square extended from Terrapin Bridge eight feet
beyond the precipice.   On this he has been seen at
almost all hours of the night, pacing to and fro, beneath
the moonlight, without the slightest apparent tremor of
nerve or hesitancy of step.   Sometimes he might be
seen sitting carelessly on the extreme end of the timber
—sometimes hanging beneath it by his hands and feet.
Although exquisitely sensitive in his social habits, he
seems to have been without an apprehension of danger.
After residing on Goat Island two winters, he crossed
Bath Island Bridge, and built him a rude cabin of boards
at Point View, near the American Fall.   Although
brought into the immediate neighborhood of the villagers,
he held but little intercourse with them; sometimes,
indeed, refusing to break silence by oral communication.
However, he was at times extremely affable to all, easily
drawn into conversation, and supporting it with a regard
to conventionalism, and a grace and accuracy of expression that threw a charm over the most trivial subject of
remark.

The late Judge De Veaux was perhaps the only person
with whom he was really familiar.   With him he would

often interchange arguments, by the hour, on some point of theology—his favorite topic of discussion. His views on this subject were by no means stable; but as far as they assumed a definite form they seemed nearly akin to those held by the Society of Friends. But it was in his brilliant reminiscences of foreign lands and scenes that he was especially glorious. He had wandered among the ruins of Asia and Greece, and studied the trophies of art in the celebrated picture galleries of Italy.

Of music he was passionately fond, and played his own compositions, in the opinion of some, with exquisite taste; while others declare his execution to have been only mediocre, if not absolutely inferior.

Every day, after his removal to the main-land, it was his custom to descend the ferry stairs to bathe in the river below; and it was while thus engaged that he was accidentally drowned, June 10, 1841 Ten days afterward his body was found at the outlet of the river and brought back to the village, where it was committed to the earth in sight of the scenes he so much loved.

After his decease a number of citizens repaired to his cabin to take charge of his effects. Little, however, was to be found: his faithful dog guarded the door; his cat lay on the lounge, and his books and music were scattered around the room. Writing was sought for in vain. It is said, notwithstanding, that he wrote much, but always in Latin, and committed his productions to the flames almost as soon as composed.

Members of his family have, since his death, visited Niagara, from whom we learn only that Francis was a son of the late John Abbott, of Plymouth, England, a

member of the Society of Friends, and that in his youth
he alternated the most indefatigable devotion to his
studies with the most excessive dissipations of a gay
metropolis.

We have given only what we *know* of his life. There
still remains a wide margin which each may fill up as best
suits himself, with the speculations of romance.

INCIDENTS AND CASUALTIES.

The number of victims whom carelessness or folly has
sent over the Falls is much larger than an ancient Indian
tradition (which says the spirit of the Cataract claims
annually two victims) would lead us to suppose.

In 1810 the boat *Independence*, laden with salt, filled
and sunk while crossing to Chippewa; the captain and
two of the crew went over the Falls.

In 1821 two men in a scow were drawn into the current
and went over.

In 1825 two men and boat, from Grand Island, went
over; in the same year three men in three different
canoes went over.

In 1841 two men engaged in smuggling—boat capsized
in the current. One was found dead on Grass Island, the
other went over the Falls. Also, two men in a scow,
boating sand, went over.

In 1847 a boy, aged 14, attempting to row across was
drawn into the current and went over.

In 1848 a man was seen to pass under Goat Island
Bridge, close to the shore, and was heard distinctly to
ask, "Can I be saved?" Soon after his boat upset and
he went over; he was never seen afterward. In the same
year two children, a boy and a girl, were playing in a skiff
which swung off from the shore. As they were rapidly

passing to the fatal plunge, the frantic mother rushed into the stream and succeeded in rescuing the girl, the boy sitting in the bottom of the skiff, with a hand on each side, went over.

The next incident we shall relate occurred on the nineteenth of July, 1853, and was witnessed by thousands of horror-stricken spectators. Early in the morning a man was discovered in the middle of the American rapids about thirty rods below Goat Island Bridge. He was clinging to a log which had lodged against a rock; he proved to be a Mr. Avery, who, in attempting to cross the river above, had been drawn into the rapids; his boat is supposed to have struck the log and been overturned and by extraordinary good fortune he had been enabled to cling to the log. A large crowd soon gathered on the shore and bridge. A sign painted in large letters "We will save you" was fastened to a building that the reading might cheer and encourage him. Boats and ropes were provided. The first boat filled and sunk just before reaching him. The next, a life-boat which had been procured from Buffalo, reached the log, was dashed off by the re-acting waters and sank beside him. Another light clinker-boat reached him just right, but in some unaccountable manner, the rope got caught between the rock and the log. It was impossible to loosen it; poor Avery tugged and worked at it with the strength of despair; the citizens above pulled at the rope until it broke. By this time a raft had been constructed with a strong cask attached to each corner and ropes so arranged that Avery might tie himself to it. It was lowered and reached him safely. He got on and seized the ropes; the rescuers moved across the lower part of Bath Island, drawing in the rope, and the raft swinging easily toward Goat Island. But when it reached the head of Chapin's Island the rope got caught in the rocks and all efforts to loosen it were ineffectual. Another boat was launched and let down the stream; it reached the raft all right, and Avery, in his eagerness to seize it, dropped the ropes he had been holding, stepped to the top of the raft with his hands extended to catch the boat, when the former seemed by his weight to be settled in the water, and just missing his hold, he was swept into the rapids, went down the north side of Chapin's Island, and almost in reach of it, in water so shallow that he rose to his feet, threw up his hands in despair, fell backward and went over the Fall. after a terrific struggle with death which lasted eighteen hours.

In August, 1844, a gentleman was washed off a rock near the Cave of the Winds. He had ventured to step onto this rock in direct opposition to the remonstrances of the guide.

In 1846 another fell forty feet from a rock below the Cave of the Winds and was instantly killed.

Perhaps the saddest fate of all was that which befell two estimable young people, residents of the Falls. On Monday, August 9, 1875, Miss Lottie Philpott, with two brothers, a sister-in-law, and Mr. Ethelbert Parsons, descended the Biddle staircase, and with merry laughter, passed through the Cave of the Winds and climbed over the rocks toward the American Fall. The members of the party gave themselves up to the keen enjoyment of bathing in the sheltered eddies and in the lighter currents that sweep between and over the massive rocks below. With a rash, venturesome spirit, Miss Lottie chose one of the most dangerous currents near in which to bathe. Mr. Parsons, noticing her dangerous position, descended to her side, and while seeking for a firm foothold for himself to guard against any possible mishap to either, the lady lost her footing and fell. Mr. Parsons grasped for her, but failing to catch her he slipped into the current and both were carried down the stream and over a fall some ten or twelve feet high. Miss Lottie found a footing in the eddy below and was seen standing in the seething waters leaning against a huge boulder. It is not known whether she could have maintained her footing here, or not, long enough for assistance to have been rendered by those on the rocks nearer the shore. If she could, it is thought she might have been saved. When Mr. Parsons rose to the surface after his plunge over the little fall he was seen to swim towards the lady, put his arm around her waist, and together, both swimming strongly, they struck out for the rocks on the other side, which, could they have reached, would have afforded a vantage ground from which successful efforts could have been made to reach a place of safety. Desperately the brave man labored to save her for whom he had ventured his life, but the remorseless current rapidly carried them down and out from shore, further and further, into the river, he swimming on his back and supporting her until suddenly they were parted. Those who were watching the scene, unable to render any assistance, say that Miss Lottie, who had one hand on his shoulder and evidently felt that both could not be saved, and that he might save himself if not burthened with her, suddenly pushed him from her, and, throwing up her arms despairingly above her head, sank below the surface and disappeared from sight. Quick as thought the noble man turned and dived for the sinking girl. A cloud of mist hid the scene of disaster for a moment and when the horror-stricken witnesses next looked for their loved ones the angry waters gave no sign of the tragedy just enacted. Both bodies were subsequently recovered at the Whirlpool.

Since that time Niagara has had several victims, two of which were unmistakably suicides; the last being a young man, unknown, respectably dressed, who, after paying his fare at the Prospect Park gate and passing a few rods down the bank, of the river, deliberately waded in and swam towards the awful brink. He was supposed to be a school-teacher, as from his description a man said he believed it was his brother who had left home a few days before.

The above list is but a partial one of known victims. The number of those unfortunates who have taken the fatal plunge at night, unseen save by the "Eye that sleepeth not," can never be ascertained.

Many have stated that when looking down from the brink into the tremendous chasm, an almost irresistible impulse beset them to leap into the fearful flood. We have never heard this explained, and why such a feeling should possess the mind is beyond our comprehension, though certain it is that such a feeling does exist in the minds of many.

THE VILLAGE OF NIAGARA FALLS.

The village of Niagara Falls contains a population of 3,700.. It boasts of several hotels, large stores, churches to the number of six (one unfinished), and has one of the largest paper mills in the State, a pulp mill, cabinet and carpenter shops, blacksmiths, wheelwrights, and everything in fact that a much larger place often lacks.

The churches, which should come first on the list, are the Baptist, Episcopal, Methodist, Presbyterian and

Roman Catholic. Of these the oldest is the Presbyterian, and the latest, finished and occupied, the Methodist, although the new building, not yet completed, of the Episcopalians, is the last. Of the hotels, suffice it to say they are quite up to the mark and range from a first-class hotel to a third or fourth rate, and their charges per diem vary from $2.00 to $4.50. The principal of these hotels are to be found on Main street, viz., the Cataract and International. The Spencer House, directly opposite the N. Y. C. & H. R. R. R. Depot, on Falls street, and the Niagara House, on Main street, are the only first-class hotels open all the year round. The main business street of the village is Falls street, down which the visitor goes on his way to the great cataract; on this street may be found hardware, dry goods, and almost all the business of the place; the post-office is located about the center of the street, and at its foot may be seen the new Soldiers' Monument.

In summer time the streets present quite an animated appearance; they are broad and well kept, and abound in fine shade trees; especially may this be said of First street, on which four of the six churches are situated in close proximity to each oth' Buffalo street contains some fine residences; on th... street may be seen the homes of the Porter family, the proprietors of Goat Island. The residence of the late Col. Porter, and also that of his son, stand side by side on this street.

There are two railway depots: one is the N. Y. C. & H. R. R. R., on Falls street; the other, the Erie, is some half-mile further, on Erie street. Carriages in abundance may be procured at either of these depots or at the hotels. Omnibusses run from each hotel, with porters, to each train, arriving or departing. Should the visitor have any objection to staying at a hotel, private boarding houses abound, whose charges vary from $6.00 to $10.00 per week.

As a whole, the charge for living at the Falls will compare very favorably with any other watering place in the United States. In addition to the above hotels, there are, on the Canada side of the river, the Clifton House, Prospect House, Front View House and Victoria Hall Hotel.

RATES OF TOLL.

Goat Island...	$ .50
Cave of the Winds......................................	1.00
Prospect Park..	.25
Inclined Railway.......................................	.25
Shadow of the Rock.....................................	1.00
New Suspension Bridge..................................	.25
Ferry	.25
Behind Sheet of Water (Table Rock)....................	1.00
Burning Spring..	.50
Railway Bridge over and back..........................	.50
Whirlpool Rapids......................................	.50
Whirlpool...	.50